i CAN'T BReAThE

JO MUET – ATMAN

First Edition: 2025
ISBN 979-8-218-64950-0
Published by Jo Muet–Atman

All poems in this collection are works of original creation by the author. Any resemblance to real persons, living or dead, or actual events is purely coincidental.

For permissions or inquiries, please contact:
www.jomuet.com or Info@JoMuet.com

Printed in the United States of America

For my Mother

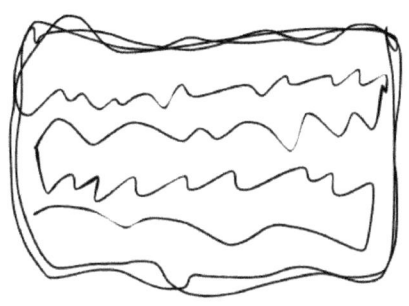

there are even words that I would not
put down on paper
even memories, you can train your
brain to forget

TABLE OF CONTENTS

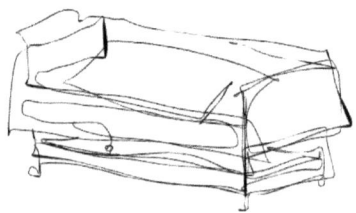

you couldn't breathe
your lungs gave out

you couldn't breathe
your lungs gave out

you couldn't breathe
your lungs gave out

you couldn't breathe

without you
who am I

without you
who am I

without you
who am I

but I can't
possibly be mad

when me and
azreal are friends

and I kiss your lips
the same as mine
and I learn to love
your scars with time

and I remember the pomegranates
by the poolside
and the fresh watermelon
on saturday nights

and I don't recall living to die
because all I do
is die to live

and when I stand on the mountain top
with clouds below my feet
and scream
I can't breathe

I don't feel what you felt
but my body does loosen
till it's
easier to see

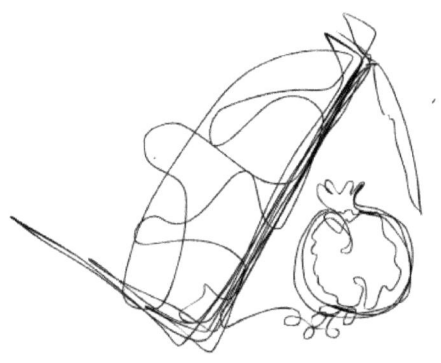

I can't breathe
but once I could
while eating pomegranates
by the poolside

with you inside
yelling at me to not dirty the knife
I said I wouldn't
but I did

now we both can't breathe at night.

it's the black shined shoes on the subway
it's the dirty looks through squinted eyes
it's the way I can't speak
it's the way I want to curl up and
it's the way you said to change my mentality
it's the way I cried as I tried
it's the way the rain hit the pavement
it's the way I write this at night
it's the way I can't breathe on my own
it's the way the green pumps me to life
it's the way I smile at the man who says
he can show me a good time
it's the way I frown at my reflection as I pull out the knife

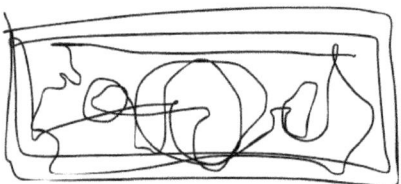

remove
the smile
the clothes
the hair
the chin
the cheeks
the heart
the teeth
the lips
and I'm just a liver with childhood memories

they said you're not gone
they said I would see you
in the trees
in the wind
in the weed
they said you didn't leave
you just morphed
into the grass
into the birds
into the cry of orphans
they said you didn't die
you just became the sweetness of candies
you just became the bitter in memories
you just became the duckling in the lake
but I would know

I would know
if you were the roots in sunflowers
if you were the peach on the tree
if you were the mom of the duckling
I would know
and I know
that you're not fucking here
you're not in the sunrise
you're not in the aesthetic
you're not in me
you're not fucking here
all I asked for was the truth

when I figure out the meaning of life
I will let you know
I won't gate keep the
truth

I promise
if you entrust me
with the meaning of life
I will tell you everything I know

I won't say I have something to share
and then die before I say it

I'll say it right there

but if I am honest
I think I will appear the same

I think I will still appear
as if I am
a starving painter
but not a poor one

I think I will still appear
to have spilt the milk
just before I was able to
clear the papers

I think I will appear the same
and everybody knows
that everybody prefers
someone to deliver such news
with some type of something

so, the meaning of life
will not be entrusted
to the girl
who appears
to have a hard time being

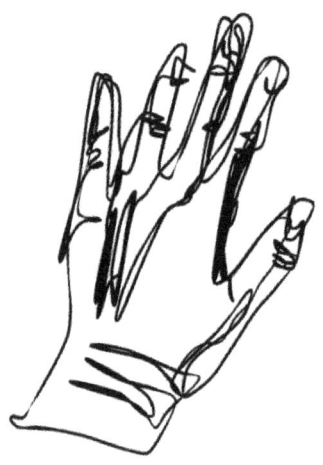

long pale fingers
pull me back to reality
as I watch the cloak
take another victim
into the roundabout of mother
for a once again ride
and when I look down at my own
short hairy claws
I tear out my hair
as I am no
better than anyone
and yet
my morals are the deciding factor
of their very similar days
and these morals of mine will fail
as I continue to tear out my hair
in fear of the day
of seeing scratches on my skin
in fear of the day
of feeling hair along my
shins

say her name
they scream
but I can't
I can't
breathe
say her name
they scream
and I shake my head
on the platform
looking out at the voices
some purple
some green
some blue
some red
and they scream again
in cursive and odd numbers

say her name
  and they watch
    they watch
      as I fall to my knees
        gasping
          gasping
            for air
              and they whisper
                say her name
                  and my lungs start to collapse
                    as I try to reach up somewhere for air
                      and they scream
                        say her name
                          and with my last dying breath
                            I say
                              I can't breathe

a consuming
encompassing
tired washes over my mind
and takes away
all the creativity I have
and takes away
all the will I once had
and leaves me
chained to an idea
that was once created for freedom
but now keeps me in isolated darkness
who next will say

"why is she weak?"

I thought of you today
and wondered if maybe
you thought of me too

I thought about how beautiful, you are
how sweet
and then I thought
maybe not that

but kind and mine
at the very least

I know you are dead
I'm not super naïve
but maybe if I pretend
then I can be deceived

because I would rather cut the trees in hell
then know
that you truly left
and had nowhere to go

laugh at me
laugh at me
laugh at me
brother isn't it funny

I wished you to blacken
with your sins
I wished that
forever wasn't in your index

I screamed at your death
I screamed
I screamed until I couldn't breathe
finally
fucking finally
I got something I wanted
a fuck you
from hell

but here I am
years later
not knowing you
not knowing me
not knowing heaven
not knowing hell
only now knowing
that you fucking won
I should have wished
for you to live – a long fucking life

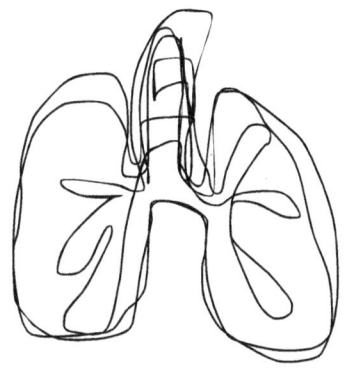

breathe

fucking breathe

bitch

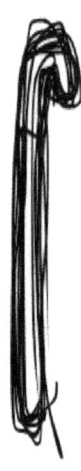

I met a man from Australia
and I fell in love
he had a wife
and a cane

but I fell in love
I wanted him
I wanted him
so fucking badly

I wanted to take him
and kiss his forehead
and wrap him
in wool

and tell him about you
tell him how much you
wanted to go to
Australia

tell him you didn't get to go
but you wanted to

I just want to
watch him breathe

you said it's not that deep
but it is
but it is

because you don't get it
you don't get it

the moth
the moth

came in from outside
for the light
for the light

but it found its way inside a hospital
inside a hospital

and I watched it
I watched it

slam itself against a bathroom door
  over and
    over

      nobody cares
        nobody cares in a hospital

        I watched
        I watched

she's dead
she's been dead, Jo
I've moved on, he's moved on and she's moved on
everybody has moved on but you
you're still sitting here
in your tears
it's been too long
you say

and I know
so I don't say anything

and you leave
I felt you leave
I think you were still there
but you left a while ago

I hang the noose
that I've built with my tears and headfirst I dive
into the cool water of grief
and my body is fighting
it wants to
needs to
come up to breathe

I buck against the lack of air in my lungs
and my brain blanks
into black
leaving one last futile attempt to save itself

but it's too late
I couldn't breathe
so my body couldn't survive

nobody's fault
nobody can breathe for me.

"they said her mother was crazy"
they whisper
and I feel the anger buzzing in my bones
with the need to scream
"she's dead. she died. months ago. she's been dead"
but it shushes me and says
"you had your chance now you may only listen"
and they say,
"her father was even crazier"
and the tears slide down my cheeks as
I open my mouth to tell
"he's dead. he died. years ago. he's been dead"
but its talons grip my shoulders as it says
"you've lost your chance"
and they say,
"she was so pretty"
and I want to bellow
that I was ugly. the whole time. my face was nice,
but I was rotten to my core.
I knew It.
but it adds chains to my legs and says
"you didn't belong here but you definitely don't
belong out there anymore, my dear"

and they say
"here lays a girl who died too young"
and my tears are heard by no one
as I follow it deeper into the darkness that I have become.

the lady was talking to you. she asked
how many children she had.
you said 6. you didn't include me? I am her daughter.
I am legally adopted. she is my mother
even if I didn't want it.
she is my mother even if she didn't want it.
it is written in by the government.

fuck you.

I stared at the mirror
and looked into my own eyes
to see if I had It:
        a soul

I've seen it leave
the eyes of people
saw the brightness leave
and didn't feel that in me

so I looked in a mirror,
into my eyes
hoping to find a soul
and what I saw

scared me

for I had the deepest hunger
deep down
with the eyes of someone
dead

I am dead inside
not a feeling
but a knowledge
I am surprised it took this long
to be quite honest
to be entirely too revealing
I would dare say I am not alone in this feeling.

what truly is life when it's spent hating your existence,
knowing that on the other half of the world there are people
who don't even have the time to sit down and examine
the fact that they have a conscious
how quite lucky I am to hate myself
how quite lucky I am to have the opportunity to kill myself
instead of being killed

do you ever pass a barber shop
possibly the one you have driven by your whole life,
possibly the one you had never seen
and just think:
wouldn't it be so depressing

if I just went in there and sat
and said to the man
"this will all be gone"
just to get a passing glance of understanding

I remember when I stopped smiling at people
nobody would smile back
nobody
I don't even think they saw me
truly.
I don't care for their smiles
but I did care for the person smiling

I would give very little to have her back
but that is because I simply do not care
she was better than me in all ways
but it is pointless to compare yourself to
someone who no longer exists

when I was younger
I told my mother
I wanted to be someone
someone famous
and then she died
and I didn't, don't, want to be anyone

not even the kid who would
look forward to trick or treating
just so she could bring candy "dots" home to her mother
just to see her mother's chapped, heartful, constant,
never-ending smile

not even the kid who would
lay down beside her in her comforting arms
when the creatures in the dark
began to look too much like people she knew

not even the kid who would
excel in school
simply because it gave
her mother something to be proud of

I would not even look at that kid
for the pure forgiveness
that child may offer me
even when looking upon me
upon who I am
upon what I became
upon everything

so, I don't and instead
I leave my ambitions behind
and sit for hours
watching the snow fall in late hours of the night
and I still see the monsters in the dark
I make eye contact
I look at them
I acknowledge them
they acknowledge me

and I whisper to the trees
"this will all be gone"
and I watch them weep

on the day of your death
I was scared it wouldn't rain
there were no clouds in the sky
the sun was bright and the lawn next door
smelled like fresh cut grass
I was scared it wouldn't rain
but it poured without a cloud in the sky

you said your parents were coming
I asked "why?"
they met her once
really not even

I begged you
to tell them no
but I only said it
with my eyes

they came for me
and I am not in the right space
to make conversation about my feelings
about how I'm doing

so I didn't
I sat there and said nothing
to everybody

you're reckless
sure, I say
you're a nonchalant danger
sure, I say
you don't like to eat
sure, I say
you don't breathe often
sure, I say
is that all you can say
she said I can't get into heaven
if I kill myself
that's where she is

Jo Muet – Atman

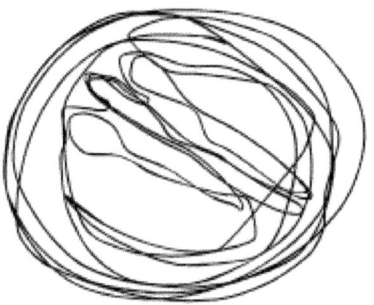

I was there
I was there
in three minutes
I was there

but I was there
too late
for you were no longer

there was a police officer
on the front lawn
I guess they were called
for the time

he watched me double park
and run in crying
this was another day for him
this was the last for me

I went to your bedroom
I cried hard when I saw you
you were in the most uncomfortable position
I had ever seen

there was a blanket over your head
I pulled it down
and there you were
dead and gone

when I was young
I would run into
your room and you would
let me sleep next to you

you never said no. never.
so, I wrapped my body around yours
and I cried
I cried for the memories I will forget
I cried for the memories I won't have
I cried for the person I will now become
I cried for the mother I will no longer have
I cried for the loss of love
I cried for the way you had died
I cried for the life you had lived
I cried for the knowledge of living without you
for the next 60 years
I cried for the lack of you as if you were a vitamin
and I will surely die without a daily intake

please do not stare
if you look over and see
me sobbing in my car
I am healing

please do not ask
how much I weigh
for I am trying to find
my worth to eat

please do not wonder
about how I changed

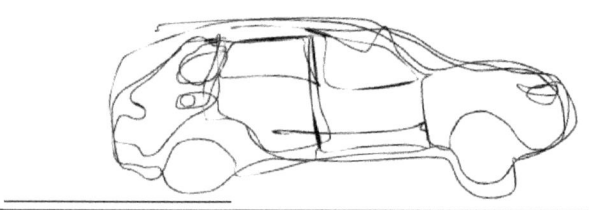

because I simply have
and now I must adapt

please do not hug me
or I will collapse
underneath the weight of compressing
every emotion I am feeling

please do not feel bad
because this is a situation
that I have dealt with and
can continue to deal with

I play sudoku with friends
but when I look up
susan is dead

God. I truly hate "how are you feeling." fucking great. thank you! I will still be at christmas. I won't lose my mind. I might stop eating but I won't kill myself. my mother is dead. no longer talking, no longer there, no more celebrating my wins, no more crying with me over my losses. no more jokes. no more advice. no more I love you. no more I'm so proud of you. no more fights. no more support. nobody else. not a single other person for me. how are you? there are no words in this language that can express my despair but if I say great you will be happy. right? god, I don't want you to be happy but I am doing great.

I can blame you for it all
I can blame you for
the pain
the emptiness
the angry
the cold
the lack of friends
the lack of family
the lack of friends
I can blame you for it all
I can blame you for it all

but you can't I scream
I stomp my foot
and slam my hands
and tear at my hair

and you look at me and say
but I can
and am

I can't process your death
because I don't have time
because I don't want to
because I can't

but I know where I am
I'm at the anger stage
and I'm angry
I'm angry at everyone

I tuck it in because I don't have space
to be angry
I can't be angry at the people close to me
I can't be angry at the person who is dead

so here I am
once again
hating myself
I didn't think it could be any more intense

you broke your arm
as I sobbed on the carpeted floor
you pushed me over
you said stop

I continued crying
pouring out songs
you sounded like her
I say

you pulled my face
to yours and
you said
you need to live

and I scream into the carpet
pouring out DNA
you look like her
I whisper

fuck, you say
you broke another arm
and with venom in your eyes
you say
you need to breathe

but she couldn't
I cry

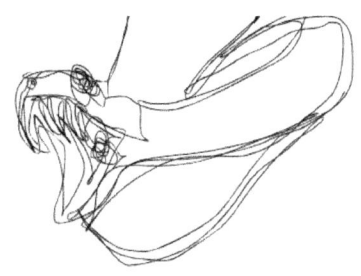

you're killing us
you're killing us
you kick me as you scream
why?

I cough up the blood
as I say
I just want her
can you find her?

you sit on the floor
your legs are broken
and as you stare at the carpeted floors
you say she's not coming

and I say
she would if she could
and you say
yeah, she would if she could.

she would if she could

I Can't Breathe

"you're happy" you say

    "thank you" I said

        "can I ask you a question?" I say

            "of course" you say

                "have you ever heard the story of Sisyphus?"

                    "no" you say

                        "don't worry about it, it's not that important"

                        I say

I'm sorry
I'm sorry
I should have stayed
I should have stayed

I knew you were going to die
and yet I still said
I'll see you in the morning
and you said I love you

I said I love you
and asked
do you want me to stay?
I knew you were going to die

no, you had said
I was late the next morning
doing an assignment
wasting my time

I got a text
I felt the floor under my body
and could only hear my screams from a
third person point of view

I lost my voice that day
I lost myself that day
I lost you that day
I lost feeling that day

and you died
and of course, I can't let you go
of course, I can't be happy for you
of course, I have to make this about me

you knew you were going to die
why wouldn't you ask me to stay
I would have stayed
I should have stayed

I would have stayed
please know I would have stayed
I would have stayed
I would have stayed
I would have stayed

It's the way I asked you
to send me what you wanted to do
three hundred and two times

it's the way
when I open up my
notes app it says
max times have been reached

it's the way I asked
why would you swallow pencils
and she said
it's all she had

it's the way
I open Instagram
and get called
tranny-pretty

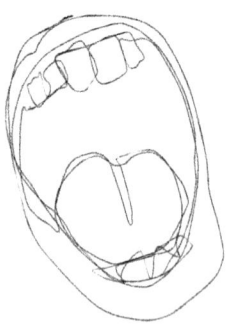

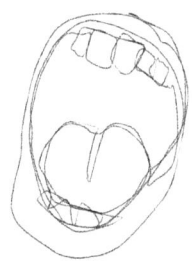

it's the way you
say it's okay
when it's not even
relevant to my words

it's the way I can't
stop being angry
over the big things
over the small things
over the constant things

it's the never-ending anger that's buried
deep within
laying on the surface
that's constantly there
in my thoughts
in my mind
in my anger there is anger

it's in the way I can't breathe
while I scream
I can't breathe

I feel your pain
in my chest
probably more than you do
right now

it's in my head
it's in my heart
it's in my soul
it's the knife in my thoughts and the
coolness in my veins

how could they do this to you?
how could life give you these cards,
this unrequited love
that I hear from you

I cannot explain this pain in words
just simply a point to my chest
and maybe if somebody cracked open
my bones
and pushed away my lungs,
a dying soul may say
what I cannot

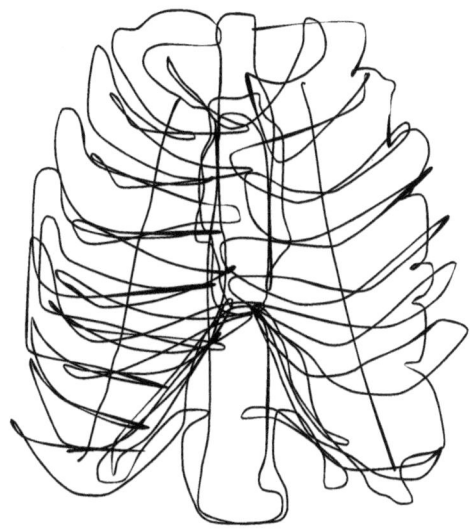

I asked you
if you were my mother
like some bad game
of guess who

and you said no
and pointed to her
from across the world
and you said

that's her

and I tilt my head
and scrunch my nose
the same as
you

and I say
I don't know her
I say
but you're my mommy?

and you shake your head
the same way as me
and you say
she gave me life

but how?
she didn't tuck me in at night
she didn't teach me to read
she didn't give me my morals
she didn't put fear of punishment into me
she didn't love me more than life
she didn't clothe me
she didn't feed me
she didn't hug me when I cried
she gave me existence
you gave me life

and you're my bones
you're not in them
you *are* them
I feel it.

it's back
it's back
baby, it's back
baby, it's back

no please
please don't look tired
please I need you
I need you for me

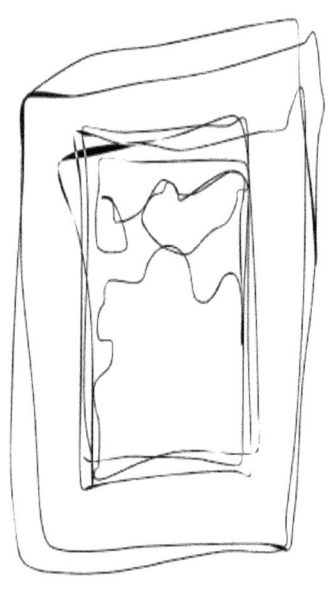

please help me
help
it's crushing
it's crushing me

in my chest
in my soul
in my mind
in my eyes
in my toes

I read once
that you're crazy if you don't
try to capture pain
with art

I can't twist this into words
I can't morph feelings into stories
I can't steal my pain for art
I can't explain this

this longing in my chest
so strong
I feel it looking for her
I feel it crying out to her

my stomach clenches
my throat constricts
my eyes haze over
the peacock runs away in fear

and I morph and morph and morph
until my ribs are connected to my knees
and my head is hiding in my bosom

and I just want to sledgehammer my soul
so that I can breathe
and you say I'm evil
you say I'm poisoned

and I know
she knows
my soul knows

christian music on sunday mornings
pigtails wrapped with ribbons
love of my life
said goodbye

kisses on my forehead
you told me to never lie
I told you
to never die

dying to say goodbye
you said don't be sly
I said don't be shy
we all liked the pie

and you prayed on the floorboards
and so did I
to a god
I hoped didn't want you

I wanted you
and you flicked my
pigtails and whispered
devil ears

and I laughed
but now I pray
they let me in
I pray they wanted you

because
what do I do with an eternity
in beauty, in color, in love
if it is without you

you said you felt him in your
heart
and I said how
I said who
I said why
I said when

you said he's in your
heart
has always
been

I said what do you feel
what is it like
Is it real
does it feel right

am I in your heart
am I in your mind
or are you just the air in my lungs
or are you just the blood in my veins

was he all you felt when you died
I didn't feel him
I hope you did
I would rather blood drip from me
then you

I'll see you in heaven
right, mom?
santa clause will be there
and maybe the easter bunny too
and they'll let me in
because I wasn't gay
right, mom?
don't say that mom
you don't have to leave right now
stay and talk to me
please
I'll get in
because I love thy mother
right, mom?
mom
don't do it
mom
don't leave
mom
mommy
I'll get into heaven with you
right, mom?
I haven't committed blasphemy
mom
what do you mean it's time?
yes mom
I do
I love you too
mom.

they're not going to let me in
mom
please
no
they won't

don't go
they don't
deserve you

mom
if you can't breathe
I can't breathe either
right, mom?

mom
mom
you'll like heaven
they'll like you
but I love you.

you said
why do you put yourself through all this pain
I said
I don't feel anything anymore

you said
that does not mean you are not going through pain
you have to acknowledge
that you are not healing
and not being the person, you can still
become

I said
you're right

and they walked away
while I've been standing in the same spot
for
three years now

Jo Muet – Atman

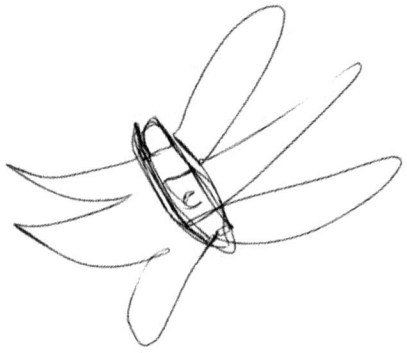

you said "she would be *proud*"
no, she fucking wouldn't

she liked me for who I was
with or
without
accomplishments

she supported me regardless
because of who I was
it doesn't matter if I became the next
self-made billionaire of the century

she wouldn't give a flying fuck
because she wouldn't
like who I
am
now

I know I don't

and the cumulus clouds
make it easier to see
but they shake me
hard

and with a plea
I ask to see
one more photo
on the tv

but as I reach out
to grab the best version of me
I lost my balance
and fall with the black

to a place I've never been
to a place where I've lost all I've ever wanted
to a place where I can't see

and I lay on the floor
with the blanket under my chin
and fall asleep by your
locked bedroom door

you hold it
over my head
like a trophy
I should kiss your feet for

your one
accomplishment
is that you've carried this weight
for twenty years now

and you want me to
to give you a gold
star of
gratitude

you want me to kiss
your wet cheeks
and wipe out
the rain

or at least say
good girl, I'm proud of you
but the honest
oven truth
is that she's dead
you're alive
and it has nothing to fucking do with you

silly me
I forgot to explain to you
what happens
if you can't breathe

you die

and silly me
I forgot to explain to me
what happens
if I can no longer see

the purpose of life
the purpose to breathe

I die

silly little me

I cried
in the parking lot
of the dentist's
office

you said you couldn't come
which is fine
not great
but fine

nobody could come
but that's fine
it is

but she would have came
she would have
she would have
dropped everything

at any time for me

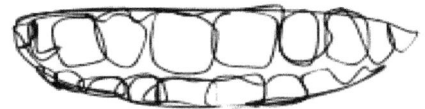

and I don't expect you to
be that because
you can't
and she's dead

the only person
with pure unconditional love
for me of all people
has perished

how fun to deal with
in the parking lot
of dentist co.

am I not a man? am I not your brother?
do I not hold the bundle of branches
well enough?

were the shelves filled with books too old,
too boring without the proper knowledge?
was my green not enough?
was it not enough?

because I did for you
I did it all for you
I gave away my clocks
I gave away my skin

it was more than blood
it was my soul
it was more than my sweat
it was my soul
it was more than tears
it was my soul

and I sit here
wanting to create something beautiful
but ugly can only create
ugly

my life is useless - I know

you say I'm important - I know

people love me - I know

I have great qualities - I know

nothing is permanent - I know

I'll feel happy again - I know

I'll reach all my goals - I know

at the end of the day my life is useless - I know

I'm sure you want to know the secret of life
how to live longer
longest
you say

and I fall to my knees
surrounded by light
I look around
and settle on you

people have killed for it
wished for it
yearned for it
learned for it
you say

and as I claw
for the ground,
I say
no

and I sit on the ground
with the lights blinding my eyes
and you
listening by my side.

what's this feeling
in my chest
in my skin
in my heart

I feel my skin crawling
I feel my stomach churning
my body is rejecting myself
it feels like

the need to constantly scream
the tortoise in the middle of the road
the death of a soul

it feels like the need to be free
from this skin
from this weight
from this quiet pain

but there's too many anchors
pinned to my skin
too many people would shed tears
over my skin

please somebody
anybody
tell me you feel this
please

but the eyes are full
and the words are
unvoiced and
the skin lacks chains

and I scream, please

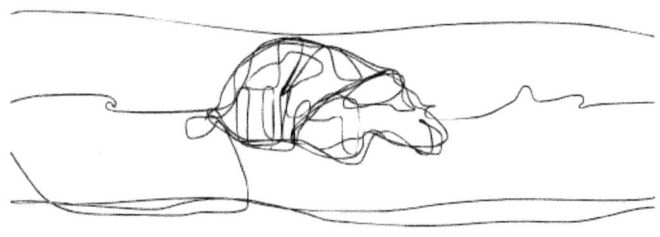

I clench my fists
and you wouldn't believe
what I said years ago

I said
I was a pacifist
I said
all I needed was to love
to be kind

and I so badly want to hit you
I hit the bed instead
and scream
and scream
and scream

and I hate your face
the same as mine
and I hate your heart
which once was kind

and I hate your lungs
which once could speak
now all they can do is scream
for someone who isn't ever coming home
for someone who... fuck it
fuck it
fuck it

nobody can understand
nobody can understand
nobody can understand
it was a piece of me

a chunk
and it's gone
it's gone
but still there
just dead

so, I can kick it everyday
just for what ifs
just for memories
that tear the rest of me out slowly

mom
they're taking me down
mom
they're taking me down

please mom
I can't
I can't live like this
without you

please mom
I'm not that horrible
I promise
mom

please
I can't do this
you're all I've wanted
all I was

but life's a bitch, right?
you live and you die
and then someone
wakes you up and
says,
"that's all you did?"

I kill the living for the dead

I pull the green from the granite

I use excess oxygen from the trees as I choke on my tears

I rip away the worms with my nails

and tell them there is nothing for them to eat

and they mock me and say

not anymore

I scare away the bugs as I scream

the wind stills

as I shriek

as I shrivel

and I scratch my skin till red

and pour dirt until it replaces the weight of you

and I kill the living for the dead.

it's not the same
she was my everything
my everything
my everything

My
Everything

I Can't Breathe

ACKNOWLEDGMENT

I would like to express my deepest gratitude to everyone for their unwavering support, encouragement, and inspiration. Special thanks to everyone for their guidance and belief in my words.

And to my readers—
thank you for taking this journey with me.

I Can't Breathe